Change is inevitable.
In a progressive country change is constant.
— Benjamin Disraeli

1. MEETING NEW CHALLENGES: EVOLUTION OF THE NONPROFIT BOARD

Boards of directors continue to be perplexing if essential parts of nonprofit organizations. Boards, after all, are required by law. One cannot start a corporation, profit-making or nonprofit, without an incorporating board. But the role of nonprofit boards is often unclear and their purposes elusive.

Boards of nonprofits often seem erratic in their effectiveness. Just when a board hits its stride, a shift in board or staff leadership, a significant change in organizational size, or a major alteration of funding or program direction can cause the board to become unfocused and unsure of its role. When this happens, the board may be viewed by the staff — and even by board members themselves — as unequal to its task or, worse, irrelevant and obstructive. Why is this so?

In my experience, a board is not and cannot be static. Instead it must change and evolve as the organization changes and grows. The roles, functions, and membership need to be altered to meet the new challenges the nonprofit organization itself confronts. Many of these changes in board roles, functions, and membership are predictable because they are natural consequences of organizational growth. It is on these predictable changes that this booklet concentrates. This essay is intended to help those nonprofit leaders whose boards perplex them and who want to clarify the board's role, purpose, and functions to improve the effectiveness of the organization.

Just as nonprofits pass through identifiable organizational stages, so do nonprofit boards. Three very different and quite distinct types of boards gradually and often quite belatedly develop as nonprofit organizations grow and change. The first of these is the organizing board, the second is the governing board, and the third is the institutional board. Undoubtedly other typical nonprofit boards as well as various permutations of these three exist, but these seem to represent three models that appear and reappear in the nonprofit world.

Before proceeding further, let me explain that I am writing principally from my own experience. I have served on 35 nonprofit boards as well as on the board of one for-profit corporation (it lasted less than a year!). I've also worked with hundreds of nonprofits in the past 25 years as a management consultant, written five other pieces on nonprofits and their boards (see the Suggested Resources section), and given dozens of seminars and workshops on boards to nonprofit boards and staffs. In the past year or so, as I have explored the ideas discussed here with clients and in seminars, staffs and boards have indicated that they have found the approach to be both clarifying and enabling.

There are, however, some caveats. The board-maturing process that I describe is not an inevitability. Organizations may develop differently, or their boards may stop at one stage or another. For example, organizations that remain unstaffed may experience few if any of the changes described below. Groups that operate in an alternative mode — collectives, for example — may also maintain a dynamic that is different and follow another path. Other boards may reach the governing stage and remain there quite happily. Still others may proceed to the institutional stage, but, lacking a clear sense of their purpose, return to the governing stage.

Indeed, because not all organizations desire or need institutional boards, achieving that final stage is not always necessary. However, if an organization's leaders depend more and more on board members for individual donor fund-raising, if the organization must serve a growing community, or if it has achieved the status of a stable community institution, its board tends to become very large and may no longer be able to function like a governing board. Reshaping board functions and roles becomes essential and in most cases, an institutional board is the result.

Regrettably, the transition from one type of board to the next, and particularly from the first-stage organizing board to the second-stage governing board, can be unclear, painful, frustrating, and laborious. If a board is to negotiate these transitions successfully, the organizational leaders must have a basic understanding of what is going on and of the changes that need to be made.

2

Leaders also need to take the time and be willing to address the issues that accompany the transition. Unfortunately that time often cannot be spared (particularly at the beginning of organizational life), without sacrificing other essential tasks or extending already outrageously long workdays. That is why the transition from one type of board may be delayed and belated; it is hard for organizational leadership to grasp what kind of change is needed and then to find the time to help bring about the necessary reforms in the board.

When organizational leaders do understand that fundamental changes are underway and that the board needs help so that it can develop, most leaders try to move the board from an informal organizing board to a much more formal, institutional, fund-raising board. They would like to skip the difficult governing-board stage where power and authority are shared, probably for the first time, between board and staff. Unfortunately, this almost universal desire to skip a stage simply does not succeed.

The governing-board model appears to be a necessary, and often prolonged, step towards the more formal institutional stage. It is at the governing-board stage that board-staff distinctions become clearer and the board develops a sense of itself and its role. Yet many nonprofit leaders find themselves frustrated and discouraged when the board does not move quickly from an organizing board to an institutional board and carry out the fund-raising tasks that leadership wants.

If changing boards can be such a painful struggle, why bother with it? I believe that developing and clarifying the board's role is essential because the board of director's involvement, commitment, sense of partnership, and strength make the critical difference in an organization's ability to continue and to grow. Executive directors and staffs — the transients in the nonprofit world — come and go, but strong boards that infuse membership with new blood on a regular basis are the constants and can provide the stability needed in organizational life. Moreover, only boards are capable of selecting new leadership, holding the organization accountable, and serving as the principal guardian of the nonprofit organization's welfare.

I trust that these brief descriptions of nonprofit board types will enable readers and organizational leaders to deal with some of the perplexities and frustrations that confront all of us as we try to make boards more effective.

2. THE FIRST STAGE: AN ORGANIZING BOARD OF VOLUNTEERS

Organizing boards are discussed in my paper *The Board of Directors "Is" A Problem: Exploring the Concept of the Following and Leading Boards* (see Suggested Resources). The essential point is that organizing boards tend to take one of two forms: following boards that are selected by a leader who wants to start an organization and who wants to create a supportive board, or, conversely, leading or controlling boards that are formed by volunteers who gather together to begin work on a mutually agreed project and then form a corporate board.

Organizing Boards that Follow the Leader

Following boards are usually small, often because the leader who invites the members to join the board does not really need or want a large board, one which might not be unified or might step out of its supportive, cheerleading role. These boards tend to be homogeneous as well, as they are composed of those people the leader knows well and trusts and whose interests are akin to the leader's. Board meetings and relationships tend to be informal with members quite content to hear reports of the organization's activities, to advise, and to offer encouragement.

Sometimes — but not always — the leader asks board members to undertake tasks for the agency and, if so, no one questions whether this is an appropriate board task or really a job for staff. At the organizing stage, such distinctions are neither clear nor meaningful. More often than not, however, jobs assigned to following board members are left undone. Board members usually have figured out that what they neglect to do, the leader will pick up and complete.

Following boards normally share a strong commitment to the organization's purpose and, probably more importantly, to the vision of its leader; otherwise it is most unlikely they would have been asked — or would have agreed — to join the organizing board. Following boards are generally not task-oriented; people do not join the board because they want to volunteer their time, energy, and skills in order to undertake programmatic or administrative tasks for the organization.

Rather, they join to support a leader who is deeply committed to achieving the organization's purpose. Probably as a consequence of their relatively passive role and of the strong role of the leader, following boards usually do not develop as intense a sense of ownership of the organization as the boards described below. Following boards, for example, do not usually play a significant role in fundraising. Generally they expect their leader to do that job as a part of the leadership responsibility.

Organizing Boards that Lead or Control the Organization

The other typical kind of organizing boards are those that create an organization and assume a strong and active leadership role. These boards are often composed of a determined band of warriors who join together to give their time and energy to a cause to which they share a passionate commitment. Leading boards may be small at the beginning and usually quite homogeneous, and made up of like-minded souls who are explicitly willing to do the tasks, however mundane, needed to get the organization up and running.

As task-oriented boards, they quickly develop a strong sense of ownership of the organization: "We got it started, made it work successfully at the beginning and it is ours to do with as we see fit." Unlike following boards, leading boards generally play a major role in raising funds, which increases their sense of ownership of the organization.

Even when the organization grows, leading boards may wait some time before hiring any staff, both because the board members are attached to their volunteer work and because they are often apprehensive about hiring staff. That apprehension probably has at least three basic causes: first, volunteer board members fear that a hired staff person may take from them the tasks they enjoy. Second, they are quite reluctant to share the power and authority that has been theirs alone. Third, often several of the founding board members would like to be the staff leader of the organization and thus paid for their services. The board then may hesitate to choose among fellow board members, fearing that it will split the board and the organization. This hesitation often delays hiring long after a staff is clearly needed.

When a staff person is finally hired, it is clear from the outset that this person is not the leader but an employee, someone who is expected to follow the board's lead and implement its mandates. Volunteer board members tend to be quite ambivalent about whether they want the staff to take charge so that they can perform fewer tasks, or whether they want to maintain control over the organization and continue to perform their volunteer tasks. Usually they want both; more help with their tasks while controlling their execution. Inevitably, staff faces a difficult situation, particularly as board members often serve as volunteer staff members, thus both working for and supervising the executive.

As might be expected, new staff leaders, even if they are willing to work hard, may have to wait for some time before they are trusted and can become effective executive directors. As long as founders remain on the board, progress toward significant staff leadership is usually difficult and frustrating; in addition, newer board members — at any board stage — may not find ways to participate effectively as long as the founder or founders remain on the board.

3. THE TRANSITION TO A VOLUNTEER GOVERNING BOARD

Despite the dramatic difference in the dynamics of these two types of boards, all organizing boards tend to be *small*, quite *homogeneous*, rather *informal* in operational style, and very *committed* to the purpose of the organization. But as the organization continues to grow, the organizing board itself — whether following or leading — begins to experience strains. Sometimes these strains are brought to a head by a crisis — often a financial crisis or a struggle between staff and board leadership — but whether there is an outright crisis or not, things do not work as well for the board or the organization as they once did.

Leading boards, for example, simply cannot cope with all the tasks and assignments that are expected of a significantly enlarged organization, and the board begins to look more and more to the staff to get the work done. The staff, and particularly the executive — understanding that they must take on more work — demand more responsibility and more of a role in setting the course for the organization. Staff increasingly resents the leading board's interference, particularly individual board member's direct involvement in the organization's day-to-day work. Indeed, board members are now expected to do any nonboard volunteer work under staff supervision. Denied the role that it had played, the board struggles to define what its new role should be.

The following board, on the other hand, finds itself being asked to do more than it ever bargained for or agreed to do. Instead of simply being cheerleaders, board members are now expected by the staff

6

leader to become active fund-raisers, financial managers, planners, and committee chairs. The leader realizes that he or she needs help in managing an increasingly complex organization and that the board can be and really must be useful if the organization is to continue to prosper and grow. With some impatience, the leader presents these new expectations to the board that simply does not want to change it role or its relationship to the leader. A process of serious renegotiation begins, often generating considerable tension and some mutual exasperation as the transition to a new board phase begins.

To put it mildly, the transition from a following or a leading organizing board to a governing board is perplexing to and frustrating for both board and staff. Usually the transition does not begin in earnest until organizing members begin to leave for one reason or another and new members join the board. New board members — who bring different experiences and new expectations — seem essential to this transition, which is one reason why an organization's bylaws should fix terms of office and limit the number of consecutive terms for board members. But still the frustrations for both new and old board members can be intense: "What have these older board members been doing? Why have they wasted their time and not really built the organization?" Or "Who do these new people think they are? Where were they when we began the organization and what do they mean when they talk about 'new roles'?"

Whatever the impetus, both following and leading boards do eventually see the need for change and the need to act "more like boards." For both types of organizing boards, this realization leads to developing a new style of leadership, one that is shared between staffs and boards. Often the change is characterized by calls for "more systems," "clearer definition of staff and board roles," and "becoming more businesslike."

For newer board members — and those original members who have become impatient — it seems that the old dynamic will never change, yet for most original board members the pace of change seems unnecessarily accelerated. For the latter, the change can be unsettling because they do not understand what their new board roles or behaviors really are meant to be. They may be unsure that they, as individuals, will continue to have roles to play or contributions to make to the organization.

Older board members' fears may also be heightened because the new people are different; women instead of all men, minorities, business people instead of community people, wealthy people rather than those of modest income. New people, too, wonder why they were brought on as board members: "Are we tokens?" "What are we supposed to do with these strange, suspicious people who don't really want to let us in to the real working of the organization?" The passage can be frustrating and wrenching for all.

4. THE MIDDLE STAGE: THE VOLUNTEER GOVERNING BOARD

What emergent vision is the organizing board struggling to create? What perhaps most characterizes the governing board is (for leading boards) the shift from performing operational, staff-like tasks or a shift from relative inactivity and cheerleading (for following boards) to the gradual assumption of the governance of the organization and the assumption of responsibility for the organization's well-being and its longevity. The board, indeed, accepts responsibility for helping to plan and execute the organization's work, for oversight of its finances, and, in general, for accountability for its organizational integrity.

Between the board and the staff, a new and more balanced relationship and a sharing of power and authority begins. The board chair and the executive director emerge as the principal leaders and accept responsibility for ensuring that the work of the board and the staff gets done. As governing boards tend to be larger and more diversified, committees become more important, more board work is concentrated in committees and task forces, and less work is done by the board acting as a committee of the whole.

The staff accepts its accountability to the board, and the board accepts this accountability role. The board also holds itself accountable to the needs of the organization by accepting responsibility for ensuring that the organization has the resources it needs to operate.

A following board may for the first time develop a real sense of ownership of the organization. The board is now expected to form standing committees that approve the organization's budget, review its finances, undertake program planning, and articulate a fundraising strategy. A leading board may for the first time trust the staff and its leader to take responsibility for administration of the organization's affairs. Board members are expected to get out of operations, hold the executive accountable, allow the executive director to manage the staff, and, in general, assume a more armslength governance stance.

Boards at this middle stage generally become larger, although the growth may be gradual and, unfortunately, not very intentional. While most small boards come to realize that governing an organization requires more people to help carry out the board's responsibilities in finance, policy-setting, and development, the search for new members is often unfocused. Instead of carefully defining the board's needs and targeting the search for new members, too often there are rushed efforts to find "good people" or the "right names."

If the board recruitment and selection process is reasonably planned and thought through, the board becomes more diverse in order to ensure outreach beyond the homogeneous community that spawned it. Like-minded, similarly motivated, and — usually — socially unified boards consciously seek others who represent and relate to other groups and communities and who bring to the board's deliberations new and different points of view. Increasing the board's size and diversity can be difficult steps for boards to undertake and accept. What had been a small, tight group is no longer one — although some board members may try to retain control within a core group or inner circle — and the search for a new, workable dynamic begins in earnest.

Committees become essential to effective board functioning. For example, planning becomes at least an informal part of the board's work, particularly as planning offers an opportunity to develop organization-wide policies that the board approves and to which the staff must adhere. A planning committee takes on this work. Financial management becomes a principal focus for board activity, and another committee accepts this task. Job descriptions are developed and a personnel manual probably becomes a necessity, not only to ensure that personnel policies are consistent, but also to keep the board from meddling in personnel decisions; yet another committee takes on this critical assignment.

The nominating committee often becomes an especially influential instrument, one designed to analyze the board's needs for new kinds of members and to develop strategies for recruiting energetic people who will revitalize and strengthen the organization. Finally, usually at the behest of the leader, a development committee is formed to enable the board to play an increasingly significant fund-raising role, by developing policies, strategies, and schedules and participating personally in fund-raising.

The staff leader finds that the transition to a governing board that really works — in both senses of that word — requires a substantial amount of his or her time. If the board chair takes real responsibility for expanding and diversifying the board and developing a successful dynamic, the executive director may be able to spend less time on those tasks. But inevitably the building of a governing board takes more time than the executive director had imagined and, unhappily, the results of the effort are not immediately apparent in terms of increased board productivity. Committees seem to take more time and must be staffed and supported. Orientation of new board members and regular meetings with board members are necessary if the executive director is to understand board members' views, what their interests are, and what they would like — or be willing — to do.

If staff and board leadership is strong and intent on making change occur, however, the board may develop a strong, new, workable dynamic within three years — but probably not much before. When organizational leaders decide that the board must change, they can become enormously frustrated when that change is so gradual — yet that seems to be the pattern. The board seems to be the slowest part of an organization to change, and the slowest to discover and operate on a new dynamic that is relevant to the life cycle of the organization itself. This delay is not due to any ineptitude of the board members or the leaders, but usually to the fact that the board is part of the organization that leaders focus on last and least, particularly in the early stages of organizational life.

Some astute leaders do, indeed, see the need to help the board change as the organization itself changes, but most do not perceive that need early enough, and they allow the board to drift. Moreover, leaders have so much to do and are so invested in status quo — in keeping power where it is, either with the founders or with the founding executive director — that they are reluctant to let go. In addition, it is difficult to get volunteers, over whom leaders have little control, to change except at their own pace. Leaders have so much else to do that taking the time to develop a board and its new dynamic often falls far behind the organization's development.

It can be enormously helpful if, at this juncture, the board chair takes seriously the task of board development and begins to establish clear expectations for the board. In addition, it helps significantly if founders agree to depart and if experienced board members who are accustomed to and expect different dynamics are added to the board.

5. THE TRANSITION TO THE INSTITUTIONAL BOARD

Fortunately, as the governing board dynamic takes hold in an organization, the board itself becomes more self-aware, and the organization comes to understand more fully why a board is important and how it helps ensure the organization's existence. This self-awareness is important because it can help the board understand that additional subsequent transitions may be needed. Having already faced a major transition, the board may be better able to accept that it will eventually need to move on, perceive new functions, assume new responsibilities, and perform new and different roles.

But why might another transition be necessary? If the organization is successful and continues to grow, the board's importance increases and the demands made of it increase. For example, raising funds from individuals often becomes the most important component of a mature organization's resource generation. More and more, it becomes the board's responsibility, supported by a professional staff, to raise money. This development in turn often means that the board's size must be increased so that there are enough board members to do the fund-raising. Other reasons for adding to the board include the need to increase the board's representation from other communities and groups or to provide the broadened public oversight and visibility that the expanded organization now needs.

If such new tasks and responsibilities are assumed, at least two things usually occur. First, the board expands, adding new and different people to marshall more financial resources and to extend the organization's outreach. Second, the board finds it necessary to delegate to stronger and more independent committees many of the tasks for which it itself had previously assumed responsibility.

Although some members may resist the idea of altering the board's role and adding new dimensions, the transition from a governing board to an institutional and fund-raising board appears to be less painful and traumatic than the initial transition from an organizing board to a governing board. First of all, the board understands both the needs of the organization and its own particular responsibilities. Now that it has reached a more powerful level, it often provides much of the impetus for change. Second, while the executive director may feel the greatest need for a different type of board, the recognition of the need for a major shift in the board's role is more mutual. The board and staff vision of the new board is mutually and intentionally developed.

Third, the board is principally adding new functions while delegating some old ones. Unlike the earlier transition from an organizing board, the board is not being asked to reorient its work completely, and therefore the pain may not be so pronounced. The board may be apprehensive about losing its intense sense of ownership, continuing contact, and feeling of direct participation. Members may experience considerable ambivalence about delegating to major committees responsibility and authority for significant organizational tasks.

6. THE MATURE STAGE: THE INSTITUTIONAL AND FUND-RAISING BOARD

What are the characteristics of the institutional board? Mature boards are usually very large and, while diverse, generally include more people who have the capacity to give or have access to funders and donors. This board gradually becomes more prestigious and more attractive to movers and shakers within the community. The board clearly accepts the role of fund-raising and often delegates governance of the institution to an executive management committee. Finally, the board, although clearly retaining its governance role and its ultimate legal authority, takes on more of a *life of its own* as it accepts new responsibilities and roles.

Mature-stage boards often increase significantly in size to ensure that the added tasks — particularly fund-raising — can be undertaken. Major charitable, community service, and arts organizations may have boards as large as 100, but a more typical board would have 35 to 60 members. As the board focuses increasingly on fund-raising, it may also create auxiliaries such as friends or patrons or establish "advisory" committees to increase the organization's fund-raising outreach without having to expand the board even further.

The task of recruiting new members who are wealthy, or who have access to those who are, is not as difficult for the organization as it was in previous years. Once a board successfully establishes itself as a governing board and has become more diverse, it has probably brought on several new members who are capable of attracting other board members who are recognized and established in the community. These latter people normally do not have the time or inclination to involve themselves in the hard work of creating an organization or even governing it. They may have done that in the past, but now they are looking for larger arenas in which to play out their community roles. The institutional fund-raising board is thus attractive to them.

In addition, organizations that seek large boards have by now established a pattern of growth and have demonstrated their staying power. People tend to see these organizations as important community institutions, ones worth supporting. Finally, a certain prestige begins to be associated with board membership as the organization develops an aura of success and stability. People like being asked to serve with others they admire and respect. To ensure that this growth continues, those board members with the most outreach and influence often form the core of the officers and the nominating committee.

Once a board reaches a membership of 30 — perhaps even 25 — its capacity truly to govern an institution is limited simply because the board has become unwieldy and hard to manage. It is no longer a board that can meet as a whole and grasp all that is needed to govern a growing institution. Much of the work of the board is already being done in committees, and the board tends to depend upon these committees more and more, receiving, reviewing, and confirming their actions.

Most institutional boards delegate responsibility for governance to a smaller group of 12 to 15 members who are often called the executive committee. This committee meets regularly to review organizational activities, well-being, and financial stability of the institution, and makes necessary managerial decisions between board meetings. It then reports fully to the board, asking for its ratification or approval as needed and appropriate.

Mature boards clearly enjoy a relationship with the nonprofit organization different from that of the two earlier, less mature boards. Institutional boards normally have achieved greater recognition as important entities within their organizations; they have goals, targets, and expectations and they are held accountable for reaching their goals just like the staff and the executive. These boards function more independently and develop new and quite different relationships with the staff.

Fund-raising probably has now become a major, if not the principal, focus of the board's activity. Other board activities — financial oversight, governance, and policy-planning — continues to receive attention, but principally from board committees. Boards expect more and delegate more to the staff as they pay attention principally to major issues and larger institutional concerns as well as funding.

As before, these issues may include approval of the staff's budget, review of the agency's audit, examination and approval of the agency's long-range goals, and evaluation of the agency's programs and leadership. But the board appears to work principally at the pre-operational and the post-operational stages and through its committees, providing overall guidance at the beginning of initiatives and evaluations of achievements and audits of performance at the completion of work.

The mature board assumes that a professional and increasingly sophisticated staff will follow approved plans and operate the organization in a responsible manner. Indeed, the busy community leaders that the organization has attracted to its board have not the time, patience, or inclination to be significantly involved in following closely the actual operation of the organization. It is imperative, however, that an executive or an audit committee, or both, hold the staff accountable and review its work and the organization's finances on a regular, timely basis.

It perhaps needs to be said that the executive committee can be a threat to the viability and sense of ownership at earlier stages of a board's life. In those earlier stages, the executive committee is all too likely to usurp an organizing or governing board's decision-making authority, leaving non-executive committee board members feeling like rubber stamps and/or meaningless appendages. At the institutional board stage, however, where boards have more than 30 members, an executive committee becomes important as the board has become too large to provide fully the oversight the organization needs.

7. SOME QUESTIONS AND RESERVATIONS

The three boards discussed above are typical of those that permeate nonprofit life, but they are not universal. There may be significant exceptions.

First, organizing boards that are also strong leading boards and that already effectively raise funds for their organizations may go through a modified or different governing board stage. Their ownership of the organization is already strong because they started it and raised funds for it. They may be able to move to something like the institutional and fund-raising board stage without assuming all of the attributes of a working, volunteer governing board.

If this fast-forward growth is so, it would probably require three steps: first, the board and its members would need to be willing to grant more power and authority to the staff and give up day-to-day operational tasks, except under staff supervision. Second, the board would probably continue to concentrate on fund-raising as its principal task. Third, a smaller group such as an executive or management committee might be delegated responsibility for governance and oversight of financial and operational activities. This committee might also include members who would be recruited specifically to provide expert and experienced financial and management oversight.

The second exception to the three-stage board model includes advocacy and public interest organizations, which are constantly at the barricades seeking changes in society, that may not be able to develop the third-stage, institutional and fund-raising boards just described. It may be that the controversial and combative nature of their work may not be sufficiently attractive to large givers and people of prestige who will be willing to raise funds and support the organization's cause. Many cause-oriented organizations have, despite their controversial nature, become well-recognized institutions in our society, and have proved capable of attracting board members and donors from one part or another of the political spectrum.

Third, it is not a forgone conclusion that boards of all nonprofit organizations need to achieve the third, institutional-board stage. Indeed, there is considerable resistance to both the idea that the progression described is inevitable and to the naming of these boards as "institutional boards." Both the concept of inevitability and the name apparently strike sparks because many public interest, cause-oriented organizations resist the idea of becoming institutions; they often equate institutions with bureaucracy — sluggish, hierarchical, unresponsive, and inflexible. Surely there are exceptions — and yes — the title does carry baggage, but organizations that stay around will tend to develop larger boards and act much like "institutional boards," like it or not.

8. CONCLUSIONS

What does all of this mean? If there are three rather typical nonprofit board stages, as I suggest, what does that mean for nonprofit leaders and their organizations?

■ *Change as a Requisite*

I believe that it enables leaders imply to understand that boards do and must change as an organization grows. Expectations of boards at various stages in nonprofit organizational life can be sharpened and become more realistic. It is not useful to expect that following boards, for example, will jump at the chance to undertake major fund-raising and governance tasks for the leader or the organization. It is very easy to become frustrated and discouraged unless one can see that the changes needed must be appropriate to the board's stage, and that these changes are difficult, requiring considerable time and effort.

■ *Board Roles*

There is also a perplexing lack of clarity about what boards "ought to do," even when one can identify the organizational life cycle and the board's stage of growth. Why? Because boards, like the organizations themselves, carry into the new phase remnants of previous activities or of the old dynamic. In a very real sense, boards are always evolving; as they age they discard and add roles and functions, and they may find it difficult to establish just the right relationship between boards and staff. Nevertheless, the three-stage process should help to clarify what generally can and cannot be done at any point in an organization's life.

■ *The Art of the (Institutional) Board*

In addition, the large third-stage, institutional boards, often avidly desired by nonprofit leaders because they seem so ideal, present serious, ongoing challenges to nonprofit leaders. It is very difficult to maintain a sense of clear, meaningful relationships with a large board so that it continues to feel important and involved. The work of any board must convey the sense that the board is truly engaged in pursuit of a useful purpose. But it is a difficult task for any leader with a large board to ensure that board members are — and feel that they are — usefully and vitally involved with the organization's welfare.

■ *Founders Impact on Board Development*

Founder leaders, those creative visionaries who feed and enliven the nonprofit world, all too often impede the development and thus the effectiveness of their board of directors. Founders' intense sense of ownership, their fear of losing control, and their reluctance to entrust others with their organizations' mission, standards, and future, tend to keep boards of directors in a supportive, following mode far longer than is healthy for the organization. Strong, committed, and caring board leaders can help create a new dynamic, as can wise founders who learn that letting go increases their organizations' and, thus, their own reach and power.

■ *Changing Memberships: The Key to a Board's Health*

Finally, all of the above reemphasizes the importance attached to orderly rotation of board members. Bylaws should specify the length of terms and the consecutive number of terms a board member can serve. There are losses as well as gains in this process because boards lose the fine, dedicated people who started the organization and who carry its institutional memory. But change is essential to enabling the boards to keep up with the times and renewing and revitalizing them so they serve the organization well as it grows. Moreover, there appears no other way to deal with inactive members or, worse, founding members who block the reforms necessary for organizational growth. Only with fresh blood and a constant source of new energy can boards move reasonably easily through the phases necessary for the organization's growth and development.

SUGGESTED RESOURCES

Carver, John and Miriam Mayhew. *Boards That Make a Difference.* San Francisco, CA: Jossey-Bass Publishers, 1997, 246 pages.

This book outlines board design, board-staff relationships, the chief executive's role, performance monitoring, and board-management relationships. Effective policies, meeting structures, committee assignments, and leadership ideas area also reviewed.

Greiner, Larry E. "Evolution and Revolution as Organizations Grow." *Harvard Business Review.* July-August, 1972. 41:35-45.

The article describes five developmental phases organizations frequently encounter, and lists the major factors that contribute to the movement from one stage to the next. The author explains common crises that result from typical organizational growth, and argues that each developmental phase is characterized by a calm period of growth that ends with a management crisis.

Houle, Cyril O. *Governing Boards: Their Nature and Nurture.* San Francisco, CA: Jossey-Bass Publishers, 1989, 225 pages.

This comprehensive text provides practical advice, principles, and procedures on more than 40 major topics affecting boards. These topics include chief executive-board relations, evaluating the executive, and improving the quality of the board. The book includes a useful rating scale for boards.

Ingram, Richard T. *Ten Basic Responsibilities of Nonprofit Boards.* Washington, DC: National Center for Nonprofit Boards, Revised 1996, 26 pages.

Describes clearly and succinctly the key responsibilities of boards. Relevant for all nonprofits regardless of size, structure, or program interest. Booklet primarily focuses on the whole board as on entity; an appendix includes valuable list of responsibilities of individual board members.

© National Center for Nonprofit Boards

Mathiasen, Karl III. "Board Membering: What Kinds of People Make Good Board Members? What Kinds of People are Needed to Make Up A Good Board of Directors" (1986, 20 pages); "No Board of Directors is Like Any Other: Some Maxims about Boards" (1982, 9 pages); "Passages: Organization Life Cycles" (with Nancy Franco and Susan Gross, 1982, 2 pages); "The Board of Directors 'Is' A Problem: Exploring the Concept of Following and Leading Boards" (1983, 12 pages); "The Board of Directors of Nonprofit Organizations" (1977, 16 pages). Washington, DC: Management Assistance Group.

The five papers discuss the fundamental of forming and implementing governing boards (budget, policy, top management), board member issues, and the various phases that boards and nonprofit organizations experience. The papers are available from Management Assistance Group.

O'Connell, Brian. *The Board Member's Book*. New York, NY: The Foundation Center; 1985, 208 pages.

Written by one of the most prolific authors in the nonprofit field, the book provides a thorough analysis of the role and responsibilities of boards. Topics covered include board-staff relations, working with committees, *Robert's Rules of Order*, and evaluating results. Appendix includes a detailed bibliography.

Ostrowski, Michael R. "Nonprofit Boards of Directors." In *The Nonprofit Organization: Essential Reading*, edited by Gies, Ott, and Shafritz. Pacific Grove, CA: Brooks/Cole Publishing, 1990, 402 pages.

The article describes the role and functions of boards of directors, and details five key board cycles that result from organizational growth and change. Discusses legal, ethical, and general responsibilities of boards.

ABOUT THE AUTHOR

Karl Mathiasen, III is the founding director of the Management Assistance Group, in Washington, DC, which provides management counseling and organizational diagnosis to nonprofit agencies. He has previously worked with the University of North Africa Association, Brookings Institution, and the Agency for International Development. For the past twenty years, Mr. Mathiasen has worked with hundreds of nonprofit organizations providing guidance and counseling, and has served on thirty-five nonprofit boards.